T0201826

Save The
BEES

THIS EDITION
Editorial Management by Oriel Square
Produced for DK by WonderLab Group LLC
Jennifer Emmett, Erica Green, Kate Hale, *Founders*

Editors Grace Hill Smith, Libby Romero, Michaela Weglinski;
Photography Editors Kelley Miller, Annette Kiesow, Nicole DiMella;
Managing Editor Rachel Houghton; **Designers** Project Design Company;
Researcher Michelle Harris; **Copy Editor** Lori Merritt; **Indexer** Connie Binder;
Proofreader Larry Shea; **Reading Specialist** Dr. Jennifer Albro; **Curriculum Specialist** Elaine Larson

Published in the United States by DK Publishing
1745 Broadway, 20th Floor, New York, NY 10019

Copyright © 2023 Dorling Kindersley Limited
DK, a Division of Penguin Random House LLC
23 24 25 26 10 9 8 7 6 5 4 3 2 1
001-333908-June/2023

All rights reserved.
Without limiting the rights under the copyright reserved above, no part of this publication may be reproduced, stored in or
introduced into a retrieval system, or transmitted, in any form, or by any means (electronic, mechanical, photocopying,
recording, or otherwise), without the prior written permission of the copyright owner.
Published in Great Britain by Dorling Kindersley Limited

A catalog record for this book
is available from the Library of Congress.
HC ISBN: 978-0-7440-7214-3
PB ISBN: 978-0-7440-7215-0

DK books are available at special discounts when purchased in bulk for sales promotions, premiums,
fundraising, or educational use. For details, contact: DK Publishing Special Markets,
1745 Broadway, 20th Floor, New York, NY 10019
SpecialSales@dk.com

Printed and bound in China

The publisher would like to thank the following for their kind permission to reproduce their images:
a=above; c=center; b=below; l=left; r=right; t=top; b/g=background

123RF.com: Actionsports 18-9, Subrata Chakraborty 14-15, Warut Chinsai / joey333 1c, 14bc, Teerayut Ninsiri 1bl,
Daniel Prudek 16bc; **Alamy Stock Photo:** Biosphoto / Michel Rauch 22, Bob Gibbons 5, Natural History Collection 7br,
Natural History Museum, London 5bc; **Dreamstime.com:** Anest 9c, Antonel 10cb (x3), Decha Anunthanapong 17br,
Bambulla 19br, Betty4240 11clb, Lucila De Avila Castilho 21bl, Dani Daniar 7cra, Designua 12c, Kirstin Erickson 3cb,
Domiciano Pablo Romero Franco 23cla, Ken Griffiths 10br, Hkratky 12-13, Ihor Hvozdetskij 23cl, Dmitry Kalinovsky 18crb,
Maigi 19bc, PeterWaters 6bc, 9bl, 10cra, 23cla/1, Sandmanx 10-11, Suttipong Sutiratanachai 8-9, Tuthelens 15clb,
Ana Vasileva 20bc, Henk Wallays 6c, 13bl, 23clb, Yurikr 20-21; **Fotolia:** Norman Pogson 17bc;
Getty Images / iStock: Heather Broccard-Bell 7cb, E+ / Mindful Media 21ca, E+ / stocknroll 21br, Joesboy 6-7,
Petia_St 16-17; **Krystle Hickman:** 5ca; naturepl.com: Clay Bolt 4; **Shutterstock.com:** Ausnative 8bc,
OnTheCoastPhotography 11c, QiuJu Song 11bc, V-yan 4br

Cover image: *Front:* **Dreamstime.com:** Mkoudis

All other images © Dorling Kindersley
For more information see: www.dkimages.com

For the curious
www.dk.com

Save The
BEES

Ruth A. Musgrave

There are many kinds of bees.
Some bees are big.

big bee

Some are small.

small bee

Bees come in many colors.
There are blue bees, green bees, and yellow bees.

hair

Some bees have a lot of hair.

hair

All bees have six legs.
They fly with their
wings.

wings

eyes

Bees look for food with their eyes.

legs

eyes

What is all the buzz about bees?

flowers

Bees have a big job.
They help flowers grow.

Flowers make pollen.
Flowers need pollen
from other flowers to
grow.

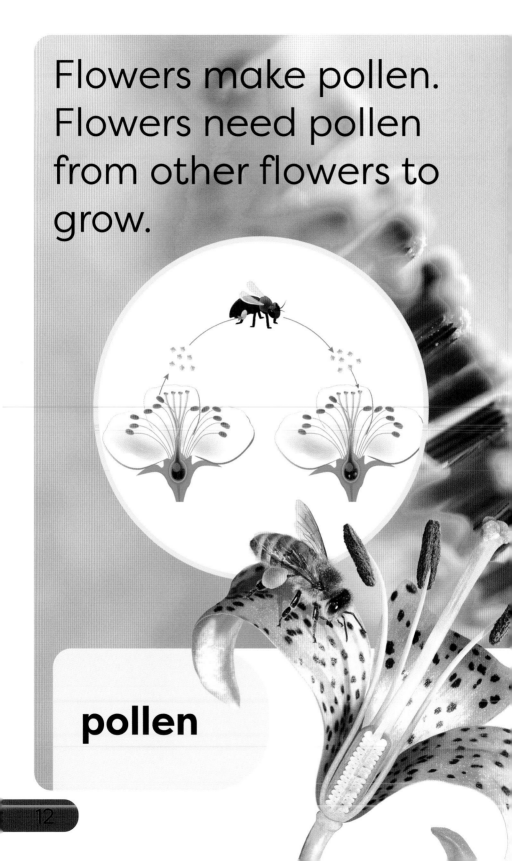

pollen

Bees carry pollen from flower to flower.

pollen

Bees carry pollen
back to their hive, too.
It is food
for baby bees.

pollen

beehive

This is a honeybee.
Look at that long
tongue!
All bees drink sweet
juice from flowers.
Honeybees use it to
make honey.

tongue

tongue

Bees need your help.
We do things that
are bad for bees.
We take away plants
they need.
We use things that
hurt bees.

bad for bees

You can help bees.
Plant flowers that
bees like.
Keep some weeds
in your yard.
Bees like them, too.
Do not use things
that make bees sick.

flowers

Bees need flowers.
Flowers need bees.
Bees need you
to keep them safe.

Glossary

bee
an insect

hair
hair helps bees gather
pollen. The pollen sticks
to their hair.

honeybee
a kind of bee that
makes honey

pollen
a powder made
by flowers

wings
bees have four wings,
two front and two back

Quiz

Answer the questions to see what you have learned. Check your answers with an adult.

1. How many legs does a bee have?

2. What is bees' big job?

3. What do bees carry from flower to flower?

4. What do baby bees eat?

5. What do honeybees make?

1. Six 2. They help flowers grow 3. Pollen 4. Pollen 5. Honey